I0480297

The Secret To Business Survival Planning

Ken Parson

Copyright © 2017 Ken Parson

ISBN:1974399737
ISBN-13:9781974399734

CONTENTS

ACKNOWLEDGMENTS

I'd like to acknowledge my dear wife Lydia. She battled through a very tough health event which ultimately has brought me to this point in my professional career. I'd also like to mention my dad, Frank Parson, and Lydia's dad, Alex Boychuck. They both have had a battle with dementia. My dad passed in 2011 and my-father-in law continues to fight the good fight as I write this in August of 2017. I'd also like to mention my good friend Joe Novara, a networking guru and Business Coach who made the suggestion that I write this book one day as we met in a Panera Bread restaurant. It's all your fault, Joe. Additionally, thanks to Joe, David Prins, John Tarascio, Dave Duncklee and Jennifer Howard for your assistance in reading and critiquing my first literary effort. Thanks to Bonnie O'Quinn, Joel Levy and Donna Ray Berkelhammer for their contributions. And lastly, I would like to give credit to all of the wonderful people within the NC Triangle business community for their help, guidance and direction. Coming out of CT as a "damn Yankee", it took kind and trusting people like them to make my mission become a reality. Thank you all - there are too many to name but hopefully they all know who they are.

Introduction

When I decided to write this book I made the decision to structure it in a specific manner, and for a specific reason. First, I wanted it to be a publication that was very easy to read for any business owner, and that it would not take up a lot of time. Business owners don't have a lot of spare time on their hands and I didn't want to write a large book that they would start reading and then put down on the coffee table with the intention of finishing it when they had more spare time but never got back to it. Or worse yet, never start reading it because it looked too daunting and thick.

And as for the contents, I felt it should be written in a way that was very easy to understand. And I've always found that stories are one of the best ways to explain how something works. With that in mind, you will read about a number of events that have taken place within businesses that I think will go a long way toward explaining the importance of what you will see on the pages that follow. In fact, one of the stories you will read is that of my own family because it was the catalyst for me getting into this area of business and ultimately deciding to write this book. While all of the stories you will read are true, I have changed the names and some other minor details for the sake of privacy for the people in those stories, except for mine.

I've also included a handful of quotes along the way. I work with a highly accomplished and experienced team of professionals and they have some strong feelings as to the importance of what you will find on the following pages. I asked them if they would be willing to give me their thoughts and, thankfully, they were all glad to.

Toward the end of 2016, I was sitting with a business attorney acquaintance of mine and we were discussing Succession Planning and Business Valuations. Real riveting conversation, huh? Well, it was for us because this is a field that we are both very heavily involved it. I made the comment that I had read that it is estimated as many as 70% of business owners do not have the proper planning in place to exit their business on their own terms. They also haven't taken all of the appropriate steps to protect themselves and their business if something unexpected were to happen to a key person(s) within their company. This attorney chuckled and said, "try about 90%"!! I was amazed to hear this. I subsequently had a couple of other meetings with highly experienced & respected business attorneys, lenders, commercial insurance reps and CPAs and they were of the very same opinion. And let's face it, they are on the front lines every day working with these business owners.

So what's the issue? Why does it matter that the overwhelming majority of business owners don't have a "safety net" plan in place if life deals them a curveball? We all know that statistically speaking the likelihood of something happening is not very large. Why not just roll the dice and play the odds that nothing is going to happen? After all, it has worked up to this point. The answer is, the ramifications of an unexpected, life changing event can be catastrophic to the future of a business, its owner(s) and their family, and the employees and their families. Would you really want that responsibility resting on your shoulders when it is avoidable?

1. The Purpose

Bill and Sally were operating what was quickly becoming a very successful graphic arts business. Sally was clearly the creative side of the equation and had a natural knack for this kind of work. All of the customers loved working with her as well because she was so personable. Bill, for his part, was an outstanding sales person - he had worked for many years in the printing industry so he had many, many contacts that he could go back to, and that turned out to be a boon to their business. So their team was a match made in heaven, and somehow, they were able to coexist in the business even though they were married, no small feat. Their company, like most, struggled early on but was starting that nice ascent that businesses hit when they finally have it figured out and things are beginning to go their way. This was going to be Bill and Sally's last hurrah work wise, and the final supplement to their retirement account. The hope was to build it up to a point where they could sell it and complete their retirements plans. Unfortunately, things did not end up working out that way. Sally suffered a stroke and was hospitalized for several weeks. After that, she was moved into a rehab facility and then eventually home.

Bill ended up spending a tremendous amount of time care-giving for Sally due to the cost of those services, so between his absence in the sales department, and Sally's absence in the creative department, their business suffered greatly. Their employees had neither the relationships, knowledge or skills to keep things going on the path that they had been. In the end, the business, which had some equipment and customers, was able to be sold, but at a fraction of what it would have been had the couple been able to run it for 5-10 more years.

Solution: Bill and Sally, as co-owners, could have established some funding coverage in the way of life and/or disability insurance in the event that something happened to either of them (Key Person Insurance). By doing so, it would have given their company an infusion of money. The money could be used to make up for lost revenue, to hire & train a replacement, help with medical bills and caregiving and whatever other needs their business might need to make up for the loss of a key person.

Succession Planning. Exit Planning. Business Protection Planning. Continuation Planning. Call it what you like but the goal is the same no matter what name you use: Cashing Out of Your Business At Maximum Value & On Your Own Terms. And perhaps the biggest question is, when do you want the 'finish' to be? Are you treating your business as a 'job', something that you work at every day but when you turn 65 or 70 you just want to shut it down and call it quits? Are you trying to build the most successful business you can with the goal of selling it at age 65 or 70 (or sooner) for a great retirement income? Or maybe you are trying to position it to be passed on to your children to run with the hope that they will do the same by passing it on to their kids.

But, what if some unexpected event(s) come up along the way? Are you prepared?

Whatever your goal is if you've built a viable, sustainable business you need to take steps to protect it. There are no guarantees that what you have worked so hard to build will endure an unexpected event or any number of unexpected events.

The purpose of this book is not to make the reader an <u>expert</u> on how to successfully exit their business as well as protect it. If someone wants to become an expert on that subject there are countless books written on the subject. They come in all shapes and sizes and have words in their titles like Succession, Exit, Continuation and the like. They are typically written by accountants or attorneys and are lengthy and sometimes confusing. By the time a business owner finishes reading it, if he/she is able to get all the way through, their mindset is that it will take a lot of time & a lot of money to put the planning steps in place, and those are two things they don't necessarily have.

I am self-employed, just like most of the readers of this book are. There are things that I am good at, and things that I am not. There are subjects that I know well, and subjects that I don't. For the things that are important to my business, that I am not well educated on, I seek out assistance from experts. I am sure you do the same.

This book represents my attempt to give you and other business owners a basic understanding of what the issues are surrounding succession planning & the protection of your business. Let's face it, people don't start a business just for the sake of starting a business. It's too darn hard. They start a business for some sort of end result. In the short run, it may be the freedom of not being in a corporate environment where everything is so regimented and rigid, and they aren't given the freedom to express their creativity. In the long run, it may be that they are hoping to control their own financial destiny, a great retirement income, or want to build something that they can pass on to their children and grandchildren.

Whatever your reason was for starting a business, it is critical that you think about not just how to grow it, but how you will exit if all goes well, and how you'll protect it in the event that something unexpected arises. I compare it to what I think some financial planners do - they're so determined to build their clients wealth that they neglect to put enough protective measures in place. Does the year 2008 ring any bells?

One such financial planner that does a great job

with growth AND protection, Bonnie O'Quinn, had this comment about business owners and financial planning:

"There are few things more devastating than a poor business succession plan – and no plan at all is a poor plan. The best planning utilizes the coordination of an experienced CERTIFIED FINANCIAL PLANNER™, Attorney, and CPA. Business Succession and Estate Planning will determine the success of your legacy for your loved ones and the things you care about most. The right team of professionals can guide you through both the easy and tough decisions to form your customized road map. Make the time to develop and implement the proactive plan components. Review your plan annually and make the changes to keep it current and in compliance. A formal plan helps to ensure that the business lives on after the owner's death, illness or incapacity. If selling the business, planning can save you both time and money. Lack of planning can cost you or your loved ones a lot of money and puts at risk all you have worked so hard for and originally intended. Make the time."

It is no different with a business. In fact, I would submit that building in protective measures is even more critical for a business than an individual. Why? Because there are usually many more people dependent on the financially smooth running of the business: partners and their families, employees and their families, venders and their families, etc.. It is these people who provide the purpose for doing good succession planning.   Your goals and legacy provide the internal purpose for preparing your business. Bill and Sally's story happens more often than you might think.

2. The Numbers

You may be contemplating starting a business, or have just recently established one. Or perhaps you've been in business for many years. Whichever the case, I congratulate you for taking the steps to create an exciting and fulfilling life for yourself as a business owner.

But before we go too much further into the "hows", let's get specific about the realities of what can seriously disrupt any well-laid plans. Some figures on business startups, success/ failure and reasons for not succeeding should be explored. One thing is for sure - the numbers, and the reasons for failure vary like the weather. So who do you believe? Here's what some expert sources are saying.

According to CNBC, 400,000 business are established each year while 470,000 shut down. That's a 70,000 deficit. But according to SBA (Small Business Administration) figures, 627,000 open each year and 595,000 close, for a net gain of 32,000 annually. Keep in mind that "closures" are not necessarily failures but will also include owners retiring from a business and shutting it down.

Now for the figures on how many businesses survive vs. fail. Like business openings, the figures for business failure vary widely. If you believe numbers from, for example, Motley Fool, then you'd know that around 80% survive the first year, somewhere between 65-70% make it through their first two years and around 50% make it past five years. Further out, about 30-35% make it past ten years. On the other hand, Forbes, using Bloomberg numbers, says that 80% of businesses don't make it past 18 months. I've even heard one "credible" source say that only 4% make it past ten years. I'm not great at math but those numbers seem very far apart to me. The truth? The SBA (Small Business Administration) gives a nod (and some credibility) to The Motley Fool figures.

The point is, it is far from a slam dunk that a small business, or a business of any size, is going to survive, whether it be the first year or the tenth year. People come up with seemingly great ideas that look like a can't-miss business opportunity but for a variety of reasons their endeavor may not work out.

Now let's take a look at what the most common reasons for business failure are.* Let me caution you that these, too, vary depending on the source you believe. And they can vary for a lot of subjective reasons like market conditions, demographics, etc. But the #1 reason seems to be very consistent.

1. <u>Business Plan</u> - a poor or non-existent business plan is the #1 reason for business failure. Business plans will define both the short and long term goals of the business and the roadmap as to how it will get there. Major categories such as the market, marketing, sales, succession, exit, production, finance, inventory, etc. are all part of this comprehensive document.

2. <u>Lack of Capital</u> - when businesses run out of money it is most often a result of poor budgeting or forecasting. Often, new business owners are too aggressive with their profit expectations and find out that it can take several years before the business makes money.

3. <u>Management</u> - Often times an entrepreneur that starts a new business is very good at one or two things but lacks the skills in other areas, i.e. management. The passion that caused them to start their company can sometimes cloud judgment as to the other critical responsibilities that will rest on their shoulders. Example, a chef may be great in the kitchen, but it does not mean he knows how to run a restaurant. Ever wonder why so many restaurants fail or why their profit margin can be so slim?

4. <u>Health Reasons</u> - Even when a business has done all of the right things if an owner, partner or key person becomes incapacitated it can

spell disaster. Some businesses operate on a small margin so something like this can be very difficult to overcome.

5. <u>Unforeseen Events</u> - the best-laid plans can get derailed by something that the owner(s) had no idea was coming. Perhaps a weather event like a tornado or hurricane, the invention of a product that makes yours obsolete, a supplier running into trouble and shutting down or cutting back. It can even be a disagreement among partners that cause a separation. It's impossible to predict, but it is not impossible to prepare.

These are widely accepted as the top five reasons for business failure. Do you see a common thread throughout all of them? With proper planning, what might be a 'door closing event' for many could be just another 'event' for you. You can't prevent a health issue, or a hurricane, or a supplier closing. But you can certainly be prepared with the resources to deal with them.

3. 8 - SECOND RIDE

Living in the Raleigh-Durham-Chapel Hill area of North Carolina, I often read the Raleigh News & Observer on line.   Back in May of 2017, I came across a very interesting story in the business section. It was heart warming and gut wrenching all at the same time. A couple who ran a good old fashioned hardware store in Raleigh had been struck by a freak occurrence which nearly put them under. And had it not been for the shear kindness of their neighbors and area business owners, their business would not have survived.   The gentleman that owned the business, a man in his 50's, was cooking outside with one of those big hot oil pots, a deep fryer for things like fish, turkeys, and chickens. He was momentarily distracted and somehow the pot of hot oil spilled onto his lower body - both legs. The subsequent 3rd-degree burns put him in the hospital and out of commission from his hardware store for a number of months. His fiancee had a terrible time keeping things running because he was responsible for around 70% of the work at the store.   He knew the products inside and out, he did all of the repairs, and in general, he knew much more about the business and the customers than she did.   She commented in the article that had it not been for the generous outpouring of donations and help, the medical bills and the loss of store revenue would have sunk them because they were not at all prepared for something like this.

Solution: No one can count on friends and neighbors to provide financial assistance after an unexpected event like this. Similar to our first story, had there been a disability policy on the injured business owner, it could have provided much-needed funding to keep the store afloat and provide the money for medical treatments. Another consideration would be for the owner to have trained his fiancee in as many aspects of running the day to day business in case just such an occurrence were to happen.

Owning your own business can be like an 8-Second Bull Ride. Using this analogy, the hardware store owner got bucked off and landed hard after about "4-seconds".

Some bull riders are able to make the complete ride, 8 seconds, and others end up getting thrown off violently. The crazy thing is that there is no way to predict what is going to happen. Just when the rider thinks the bull is going to go right, he goes left. When he thinks the bull is going to go left, he goes right.

The same can be said about business. You're going along fine, sales are up and everything looks bright. You just landed a big new order for your product from your best customer and life is good. They tell you they will need the delivery in forty-five days and you tell them that is more than enough time to deliver. You excitedly call up your raw materials supplier and tell them they need to double the usual order because of your big, new contract. But then it hits. Your supplier tells you that they have had a major piece of equipment go down and between diagnosing and repairing they expect their product delivery scheduled to be set back by 30 days. You quickly do some calculations in your head: delivery from supplier to your company, production, quality check, packaging and finally delivery to your customer. The new calculations, adjusted for this new information you have, tell you that there is now no way you can meet your best customer's deadline. You contact the customer with the news and they tell you they will have to go elsewhere because they have been given a deadline by THEIR customer. Now you have lost the big, new order, and quite possibly, your best customer. Is it fair? No! But neither is a bull ride. You get on the bull (start a business), you've practiced riding and gotten into great physical shape (business planning), and then the gate opens (you open your business doors). And then the "ride" begins.

But here's the thing, getting thrown off the bull before the 8 seconds is up, and landing safely, isn't so bad, right? You don't win prize money but you're alive and well. Yes, you're alive and well but without earning prize money (profits), you won't be able to keep doing what you love (the reason you started your business). Wow, there really are a lot of similarities.

4. Who, Me?

In 2006 I had been self-employed for about three years. I was working as an insurance sales district coordinator. In this position, I had a sales team reporting to me and we were all highly dependent on each other. Most insurance agents are paid 100% based on commissions so any interruption in that can be very costly. Part of my job was to spend time training and nurturing both new and existing sales reps. And since I was paid solely on commission, the better I did my job training and helping them, the better they did their job, which meant we all made out well. And that is exactly what was going on that February day when I got a call from my wife. At least the caller ID said it was her but the voice on the other end sure did not sound like the person I knew. From what I could make out, she had just suffered a serious medical event and needed me to rush right home. When I got home we both knew that we had to get her to the hospital right away, which we did. The doctors immediately started doing their exams and reviewing her medical history, and before I knew it they had rushed her to the MRI unit. Now I knew something was up because at that hospital there is usually a one to two-week wait to get an appointment for an MRI - they took her right in. Now my heart is starting to beat a lot faster. An hour later, out of the MRI she comes, and into a waiting ambulance she goes, to be

18

transported to the larger regional hospital that can better deal with these types of cases. The next year or so is still a blur. My wife had suffered a stroke - in her case a brain bleed. She was admitted to the ICU, then the rehab wing where she spent several weeks with physical, speech and occupational therapists trying to regain all of her physical, motor and cognitive skills. And time with the doctors, of course. The recommendation was brain surgery, and as soon as possible. After seeking out a second opinion we moved her down to Durham, NC to have the surgery done at Duke Medical Center. The surgery, while very scary for the whole family, was a complete success and then the hard work was about to begin. Over the next year, my wife lived with her parents in North Carolina going to rehab 3-4 days a week and being incredibly well cared for by them. The job that my in-laws and the professional caregivers did was nothing short of miraculous. But there was a huge price being paid within our family and within my sales team. Remember the sales team and how we all got paid. We were just like any business that has employees where everyone had a job and a contribution to make. But, if you take out a key piece to that team, in this case, me, you are going to suffer some problems. And we did. Sales dropped significantly which meant income dropped significantly. Not just for me, but for the people reporting to me as well as those that I reported to. The lifestyles of many of us were very much altered, and some of the team had to make difficult decisions to leave our group. That was the income side effect.

The expense side effect was almost as difficult. The

hospital in Durham, NC was 600 miles from our home. When you need the best possible care, and after care, you do what you have to do. So that subsequent year was filled with many trips to North Carolina, extra time spent with our three children since only one parent was home, and medical bills galore. To say that our family and my business suffered a massive financial setback would be an understatement. There were times that I was not sure we were going to make it and probably would not have had it not been for the support I got from family members on both sides and friends.

Solution: A disability policy on my wife would have given us the funds to help make up for lost income, pay for faster travel (air vs. car) and make valuable business decisions to help members of my sales team.

How many of us think we are going to get sick or hurt? As a percentage, it is very small. I saw some interesting numbers once on long-term care that really speak to the denial that exists in this area. According to statistics, 50% of all Americans over age forty feel that just about everyone will need some amount of long-term care in their lifetime. But, only 25% of Americans think they will need it!!! That math does not add up. In case you're wondering, the answer as to how many Americans will require some amount of long-term care in their lifetime stands at 70%!

But my point is, there is a massive amount of denial in America that these terrible, life altering events will not happen to us. They will happen to the "other guy". But, the "other guy" is saying the same thing we are. So then, who is the "other guy"? It can happen to any of us at any time.

Denial can be a good emotion in some cases. Think about when you decided to start your business. You most likely knew that many, or most, businesses fail. But the denial that yours would fail made for the 'green light' you saw to move forward. So, denial can be a good trait at the outset but is a dangerous one when it comes to planning and thinking that nothing will ever happen to you or someone else in your company. To use hope or luck as a strategy is a big mistake.

So how does something like this hurt a company? Great question. The problem with not preparing for unexpected events is that there are so many people that could be dependent on the well being of the business owner, partner or key person. I know it is not fair to those 'key' people, but as they say, it comes with the territory. Ownership has its privileges but it also carries big responsibilities.

If a company has a solo owner and he or she goes down, decides to retire early, goes through a divorce or any number of life changing events, the fallout can be swift and far reaching. Especially if there has not been any pre-planning put in place. Who is the 2nd in command? The owner's spouse? Son? Daughter? Office Manger? Sales Manager? Who is going to fill the owner's shoes for their day to day responsibilities? How are the hours made up? Are the other employees trained to do the things that the owner did, like ordering inventory, sales, finance, etc.? When you think about it that way, the same goes if any key employee were to be lost, like the top sales person, the finance person, IT guru, production manager, and on and on. Any way you look at it there are going to be major financial, sales, production, finance and managerial issues that will have to be worked through.

OK, that takes care of the first level! Now on to level two. How about the rest of the employees and families? As was the case in my story, families that rely on the employee's income for basic necessities like food, gas, clothing, piano lessons, car payments, mortgage payments, health insurance, etc. will surely be hurt badly.

But there is more. Depending on the type of business it is, there could be a big effect on its customers. If a business suffers due to lack of proper planning, and because of it they are unable or less equipped to supply their customers, then there is another layer of affected people.

I will leave you with two very important thoughts from this chapter: <u>First, don't think it can't happen to you. It may not, but it very well could. Second, there are a lot more people affected by a business owner's lack of proper business planning than just themselves and their family.</u>

5. Had Enough Yet?

Twenty years ago, at age 46, after a successful 25-year career in the corporate world, John decided to start his own dry cleaning business. There was only one dry cleaner in his town of 30,000 so it seemed like there was plenty of room for another one. He opened his doors, and with some good solid marketing he was off and running. Everyone loved John's friendliness and his progressive ideas on providing a delivery service, eco-friendly cleaning & daily specials and it made his store an almost instant success. Things went so well, in fact, that within two years he opened up another store in a neighboring town. Two years later he added another one and then a year after that came the fourth store. About the only thing that was hard was the time and effort John had to put in to keep things running as well as he wanted them to. Business was booming but he always found it a challenge to find employees that would provide the same level of customer service as he did. Just about the time the fourth store opened John's only son, Peter, headed off to college. Peter had a keen interest in getting into the family business and John wanted nothing more than to bring him in and then eventually leave the business to him. Peter had spent many summers helping out starting with sweeping the floor and graduating to delivery and all other facets of the business. He purposely selected a college that *was well known for their business classes and also offered a five-year program whereby he could graduate with his Masters in Business Administration (MBA). Five years later, armed with an MBA and all sorts of great new knowledge in the areas of marketing, finance, sales and operations, Peter came to work in the dry cleaning stores full time. Things were working out so well with Peter working in the business that John kept giving him more and more responsibility and Peter did not disappoint. And things were going very well outside of the business for Peter as he had met a girl and their relationship became very serious. After three years of dating, Peter and his girlfriend got married. As time progressed John gave more and more responsibility to Peter, who was then working very long hours. But he was happy and the money was good, so all seemed fine. John, for his part, decided that at age 66 he was ready to remove himself from the business and formally pass it on to Peter. They met with their accountants and attorneys and set up a payment plan between Peter and John that both were satisfied with. What no one planned for was the fact that several years after ownership transferred to Peter, he and his wife would start having marital problems which would eventually lead to divorce. At that point ,the dry cleaning business was valued at $800,000 but John was still owed $500,000. Based on the laws of their state, Peter's wife was entitled to half the value of the business, $400,000. Net result? After John was paid back Peter and his wife walked away with $150,000 each and no business.*

Solution: A buy-sell agreement could have alleviated

some, or all, of these issues. Had some planning been done, at a time when heads were cool and relationships were strong, the outcome would have been dramatically different. This company also could have put a funding mechanism in place, in this case, an investment growth product, which would have allowed for available funds to make the buyout of Peter's wife possible while Peter continued to run the business.

In a perfect world, everything has a happy ending. The business is established, it then grows and multiplies in value, and then it is sold or passed on at maximum value, and on the owner's terms. Want to venture a guess as to how often that happens?

In addition to the traditional business planning we discussed in Chapter 3, which helps you grow your business, there is another critical planning area that an alarming number of business owners ignore or overlook. It's called Exit and/or Succession Planning. Because let's face it, there is a 100% chance you will be leaving your business one day.

The terms Exit Planning and Succession Planning are often misused or misrepresented, in my opinion. It's my belief that it is ALL Succession Planning!! I am a great believer in keeping things simple and when you really examine the act of getting out of your business, it all boils down to what you are going to do with it and how you will accomplish that.

Succession Planning

There are a number of different ways that an owner could leave their business and I have listed them here.

Pass On The Business to Family: There are some very interesting statistics when it comes to passing on a business or multi-generational businesses, as they are called. Less than one-third of them survive the transition from the first generation to the second. And only 50% of the remaining ones make it through the transition from the second the third generation. That means about 16% of family businesses make it to the third generation. And if that isn't cause for concern, how about the fact that about 90% of all businesses in America ARE family owned! You can see the challenge.

Transition The Business To Current Employee(s): Often times there is an employee, or multiple employees, that have an interest in purchasing the business from the original owner(s). This is a great way to 'sell' a business because of the familiarity that all parties have with one another.

Sell The Business To An Outside Party: This is a common scenario but one that can have twists and turns that can affect the amount of money you walk away with. An outside party is more apt to really negotiate hard for as low a price as possible. If you enlisted the assistance of a business broker to help find a buyer then you are going to give up something in the neighborhood of 10-20% for their services. A good business broker may be worth the price, but it's going to cost you.

<u>Employee Stock Ownership Plan:</u> This is the process of "selling" the business to ALL employees, not just one or two. While fairly uncommon in the scope of our discussion, this is a viable option under the right circumstances. With an ESOP, the owner would sell the company to an Employee Retirement Trust that would be formed. The money that the trust uses to pay the selling owner would be borrowed from a lending source, like a bank. Then the trust would pay off the loan with the lending source from future company profits. The owner walks away whole and the employees are happy because they have their jobs and profit sharing. This works particularly well with companies that have low debt and high employee retention. High debt and low employee retention does not lend itself well to ESOPs

<u>Unexpected Separation:</u> There's one other very critical scenario to consider - you or a partner leaving the business unexpectedly, possibly due to one of the following: divorce, death, disability, early retirement, etc. These are things that are not part of the three traditional exit plans but that are very real possibilities that justify taking the time to put contingency plans in place, a huge one of which is a succession plan.

Succession Planning is the process by which the owner(s) prepare 'successors' to take over the business, prepare the business to be taken over by 'successors' or protect the business from unexpected events. Keep in mind that you NEED to do this type of planning in all four scenarios that I just mentioned. However, the steps will differ depending on what you plan to do with your company, and in the less likely event that something unexpected happens to you or a partner.

In the first two cases, <u>Pass The Business On To Family</u> & <u>Transition The Business To Current Employees)</u>, the necessary planning is really pretty similar. Where it can differ is if the family member(s) that you want to pass the business on to does not currently work in your business. I would submit that you should be very careful about going down that path - that's the kind of strategy that has led many a multigenerational business to shut its doors.

Some of the steps to properly prepare family or employee(s) for taking over include, but are not limited to*:

1. **Choose Your Successor(s):** You have to start here. You need to choose a person or persons that you feel confident will continue running the business in the way that you built and developed it. It has to be someone that possesses the same kind of work ethic and

desire to provide 1st Class service to the customers. It also needs to be someone that has the vision to pivot when the market changes. When you look at how business was done and products were brought to the market twenty years ago vs. now (newspaper ads vs. social media, cassettes vs. digital music, etc.), a lot has changed and will continue to do so. Different generations want different types of products and want to be approached differently (phone vs. email or text). There are many criteria to consider when choosing a successor - just be thorough.

2. **Develop A Formal Training Plan For Your Successor:** There are many, many facets to a company. When you started your business you were there as things grew so you were exposed to all of the different departments or functions of the company. A successor most likely will not have had the same exposure so they need to get it. A good plan starts with identifying all of the key functions of the business (sales, marketing, finance, customer service, shipping, receiving, etc.) and then having the successor(s) work and train in all of these areas. It will take time, but you have it. In this process, it is wise to be mindful of the "culture" you have in your business, and presumably, want to continue. If that culture has been a successful one, and I assume it has if your business is thriving, you want to nurture that throughout this training process.

3. Establish A Timetable: It is imperative that a timetable is set up so that everyone, especially employees, knows who is in charge and when. The employees need to be a major consideration in this process because they have been used to your personality for a long time and then all of a sudden, there's a new sheriff in town.   Your efforts to sustain that culture aside, everyone has a different personality so there will be some new dynamics going into place.   The more advance notice of the changes, and WHEN they will take place, the smoother the transition will go.

4. Prepare Yourself For Retirement: It is never too early for you to take this step.   First and foremost, you would want to make sure you are on the right track financially.   Not an easy task when you have pumped your heart, soul & maybe life's savings into this business. But you need to work with a trusted financial advisor to put a plan together for this.   Other considerations for yourself include what you will do with your time (recreation, volunteer work, travel, community involvement, etc.).

5. Install Your Successor: The day has finally come and you have to let go. The toughest part of this is letting the person(s) you've trained to take over, take over. There is a huge element of trust involved here, not the least of which is trusting yourself that you've made the right decision. If you've followed the planning steps then you've done all you can do - enjoy yourself,

you did it right!!

* SCORE Developing A Succession Plan 1/3/2012

If your plan is to sell to an outside party, or form an ESOP, the most critical thing you can do is make your business very attractive to purchase. I consider this to be a 'succession plan' - you're preparing the business to pass on to someone - it just so happens that the person is not working within the confines of the company now, and you most likely do not know them.

Of utmost importance here is that you have your 'house in order'. Critical areas here include:

1. Finance: The books must be in great working order. One of the first things a potential buyer is going to do is look at the financial health of the business so it is imperative that they can easily see that. Good bookkeeping will do that for them.

2. Employees: Have you ever walked into a room full of people and gotten a feel for the environment? You get a sense that it is a room full of happy people, or unhappy people, or people that don't really care? I have. It is the same within a business. I have walked through countless businesses and in almost all cases you can tell if it is a happy culture full of people that aspire to do their best and feel an attachment to the company such that they want to help it grow and prosper. Or, if it is a culture

full of employees that just show up at work, do no more or no less than their own job, and go home when the clock strikes 5:00. Outside buyers who may be inheriting employees are going to want, and need, to see people that are more than just time clock punchers and who are invested in the business's success.

3. Cleanliness & Tidiness: It sounds basic but we only get one shot at 'first impressions'. Make sure everything looks organized, clean and can be easily accessed if needed. If it isn't, the buyer will be saying to himself, "I'm going to have to clean up this and that, rearrange this and that, force a dress code on the employees, etc. All of that equals time, money & aggravation. That goes for the inside and the outside of the operation.

4. Operations: This is a huge one and I use this term to encompass many things. Is your IT (computer) system up to date and being fully utilized? Do you have good systems in place to service and identify current as well as prospective customers. Is your production floor designed to operate efficiently? Are your people properly trained in the art of interaction with customers and prospects?

5. Product/Market: A buyer is going to do their due diligence on what product or service your business offers. Likewise, they're going to research the strength of the market to make sure there is longevity. But, the more

knowledgeable you are about both of these areas the more interested buyers will be. Obsolescence is an ugly word in business. If a buyer can be assured that your product/service and market are ready for the long haul then you have a winner.

Whatever your plan for the business is, you must make sure that you get a succession plan in place and keep it updated as things change. It may not be an easy thing to do - some egos and feelings may get hurt along the way - but after all, it is your business and you are entitled to decide how you get out of it and what you leave behind.

6. What's It Worth?

Some time back I was asked to do a Business Valuation (a small business owner wanted to know how much his company was worth) for a gentleman who owned a roofing company. He'd been in business for around 15 years and by all appearance he had been very successful. He did repairs, replacements, updates, etc. and he was very good at it. He wanted to see what his roofing company was worth because he was starting to contemplate, and plan for, retirement and spending lots of time on a roof and ladder does have its risks. We talked and discussed his business and he shared with me some facts and figures including that he grossed upwards of $250,000 annually. And seeing that he had minimal overhead - no employees, owned his equipment and vehicle, worked from his home, spouse kept the books, etc - it meant he was netting somewhere north of $200,000. That's a darn good living. I suspect his hope was that the company value was some multiple of his net earnings, perhaps 2 to 3 times, maybe more. But unfortunately I had to tell him that he really did not have a 'business', a more accurate description of what he did in roofing was a 'job'. You see, there was really no tangible assets to go with his business unless you want to count his truck, ladder, and tools. And as for intangible assets, there were none. If you have *a home cleaning business and it includes a regular client list of 50 homes that get cleaned every two weeks, then you have some assets to sell. Had this roofing business had contracts in place with insurance carriers to repair damaged roofs, or contractors to roof all of their new construction, things would be different, but it didn't. So the best advice for a business owner like this is to work with a good financial planner to invest and save as much of your income as you can to be prepared for your golden years.*

The term Valuation is a fancy way of saying 'how much is your business worth'. I am going to discuss some different types of valuations for the sake of educating the reader but the bottom line is, your business is worth whatever a buyer is willing to pay for it. Unfortunately, I find more often than not, business owners find out that their company is worth less than they thought and that can be very discouraging (and often comes later in the timeline than they would prefer).

Here are some thoughts from Joel Levy, a very prominent, small business CPA based in Chapel Hill, NC:

"Most small business owners are so busy keeping their heads above water that they don't step back and work ON their business rather than continuing to work IN their business. While many are building the business as their retirement asset, they don't take the time to plan for this eventual succession, which could certainly leave them short of their retirement goals."

Joel continues,

"One of the most important factors to begin the planning process is to have a valuation performed on your business. This will provide a realistic number, not the figure the owner has floating in his head, that the owner can use to begin his(her) planning process. This is especially critical if there is more than one owner. The idea is to make sure that the business owner is not deluding himself(herself) as to the value which could be a disaster when it is time to sell the business and move on. Unfortunately, most small business owners believe that it is worth more than it is, and if he(she) is counting on this asset to retire on, the owner could be left short of assets they need to retire in a reasonable manner."

What are the key factors when a business valuation is done? Here is a pretty comprehensive list of things that should and will be looked at.

People: What is the record of success for the existing management team? Is the success of the business overly dependent on the presence of the current owner(s)? If it is overly dependent on current owners than there could be a big hit to sales when they leave. What is the experience and commitment of the existing staff, especially key people?

Assets & Liabilities: What is the value of assets on hand (i.e. equipment, vehicles, machinery, property)? Are there enough orders lined up to keep the business busy? Is there a large amount of debt?

Intangibles: Intellectual property such as patents? The strength of customer relationships? Growth potential of the business?

External Factors: How is the economy performing? Where are interest rates at, and where are they going? How are comparable businesses being valued, and are they selling?

Finance: Past, present & projected future earning? Cash flow? Cost control? Future capital expenditure needs?

There are many different valuation methods and types, and they come with a lot of fancy financial name tags. Let me break down the 'big three' methods for you briefly so you can better understand them.

1. Asset - with this method the primary focus in determining the business value is what the material, tangible items are worth. Property, machinery, equipment, vehicles, inventory, etc. This method is often employed if the nature of the business tends toward erratic earnings or if the business is slated to no longer operate. In that sense, it almost equates more to an appraisal than a valuation. This method also generally leaves out goodwill which, in a small business, can be a very big factor.

2. <u>Income</u> - valuing a business based off of earnings, both historical and projected, is a far more common method. This method entails looking at past earnings results and giving them a weight factor with the more current figures weighed more heavily. Another version of the Income method is to look at projected future earnings and giving those a weighted value with higher weight going to the present earnings and lower as the projections go out further.

3. <u>Market</u> - This process involves looking at other comparable businesses in a similar geographic area and deriving valuations using some multiple thereof, based on the company size and other performance factors. Often times it is very difficult to use the Market approach because there may not have been a sufficient number of businesses comparable to yours sold in your geography.

Utilizing one, or all three of these methods, some valuers will use the terms 'Calculation of Value' or 'Conclusion of Value'.

<u>Calculation of Value:</u> This is done by using one of the valuation methods above and is typically used for sales or planning purposes.

<u>Conclusion of Value:</u> This is done utilizing all three of the valuation methods and is typically used for estate, IRS or divorce reasons.

It is not unusual to have multiple valuations come up dramatically different which can be a real frustration for business owners. A couple of common reasons include a different weight being put on the goodwill value of the owner and the use of different discount rates in the case of historical or future earnings. One good way to avoid ending up in this situation is to protect yourself and the business with a buy-sell agreement, make sure it is funded properly and have regular (two years) valuations, or at the very least a formula in place, for the sake of consistency.

I met with a CPA not too long ago who was working on a valuation of a business for a divorce settlement. He was working on behalf of one side and another accounting firm was working on behalf of the other. In the end, his valuation came in at approximately $300,000 while the other side was right around $900,000. As you can imagine, that differential, in a divorce settlement, can have huge ramifications, especially when they go to sell the business and it garners closer to the low figure for a purchase price.

Valuations are typically performed by CPA's and run anywhere from $3,000 to $10,000+ in cost depending on whether the owner is looking for a Calculation of Value or a Conclusion of Value. However, not all CPA's do them because they can be very time consuming, and depending on why the valuation is needed, it can draw the valuer into a legal area that they may not want to tread. Valuations play a critical role in the subject of the next chapter: Buy-Sell agreements. Having an accurate valuation, and more importantly, a valuing method that all partners and interested parties agree on can save a tremendous amount of problems down the road. It may be just a formula in your buy-sell agreement, but at least you'll be able to arrive at a figure that everyone can work with.

7. Unexpected Partner

I remember a case where a client had started a business with a college friend. Both were married and in their thirties. Death or disability seemed impossible to conceive and they figured that they had plenty of time to write a buy-sell agreement when their business was stabilized. As fate would have it, one of the friends, who owned 50 percent of the business, died tragically — leaving his wife to control his half of the company. This would not have been, in and of itself, a problem since the surviving partner cared deeply for his partner's family. Unfortunately for the future of the business, the deceased partner's wife remarried and her new husband, who had previously owned a business, felt that he could step into the deceased partner's shoes. One can only imagine the trauma caused by this situation. A negotiation for a buyout of the deceased partner's 50% was attempted but it was not possible to deal with the new "partner". After a period of about six months, it was impossible to continue as all decisions regarding the business had to be agreed upon by both of the parties. In the end, the business was liquidated for a fraction of what the company may have been worth if allowed to be operated by the surviving founder.

Solution: The way the initial partners could have avoided these problems would have been to establish a strong buy-sell agreement at the outset of the business. Although this is an extreme example of what can happen when there is no agreement, given the statistics, it is likely a more common scenario than one might believe.

A critical cornerstone to succession planning is something called a <u>Buy-Sell</u> agreement. In its most simple terms, it can be compared to a prenuptial agreement between two or more business partners. There is even a type of Buy-Sell agreement for individually owed businesses which I will touch on shortly. The Buy-Sell agreement is an essential part of business planning because it takes into account that things will most likely not always go smoothly in a new or established business. It is a document that will give the business owners a 'contingency' plan on paper. There are literally countless scenarios that can happen within a business that can derail everything you've worked to build but a well structured Buy-Sell can help virtually all of them be avoided. Had our partners in the story above had the foresight to put a plan in place they'd both be far better off.

This seems pretty logical - put a Buy-Sell in place and avoid a potential mountain of emotional and financial heartache. So why don't more business owners do this? In my opinion, it is because they have a perception that it will be very costly (legal fees) and time-consuming (meetings). The good news is that neither of those reasons has to be true - there are affordable and streamlined options that can give you the valuable protection you need. Let me pose this question: when you think of the financial value of your business, and the sweat equity that you've put into it, would it be worth spending $1,000 and a few hours of your time to protect it? I think it is safe to say that most of the readers will say yes.

Here's what Donna Ray Berkelhammer, a top business attorney in the Triangle Region of NC, has to say about the importance of having a Buy-Sell Agreement:

"One of the most difficult situations for small business owners is the "business divorce," where the owners no longer want to be in business together. The better option is to draft an agreement up front that lists events that could or must trigger a purchase of one owner's interest. These events often include death, disability, divorce, bankruptcy or incompetency. Death and disability should be funded with insurance, so there is money to pay the owner or his/her estate."

Let's move on to the different types of Buy-Sell agreements. Like Valuations, there are numerous types of buy-sell agreements with fancy names that may only serve to confuse the business owner. I will try to keep it simple:

<u>Cross Purchase</u> - this is the most common type that I see. It can be used when there are two or

more partners in a company. Since most multi owner businesses have two partners this makes this type of agreement the best option. In a Cross Purchase, the Buy-Sell is written in a way that if something unexpected happens to one of the partners, the other partner will have a chance to acquire their half of the business. It is designed to assure that ex-spouses, second husbands, children or any other unwanted, untrained or uninformed person don't become a partner with the surviving person. A proper Buy-Sell is worded to accommodate such triggering events as death, disability, divorce, early departure and even the forced removal of a partner. It also will have a section summarizing the value of the business and make accommodations for keeping that company's worth updated through either regular valuations or utilizing a formula method. These plans are often funded with life and/or disability insurance policies because they are the least expensive way to provide critical funding if something unexpected happens. More on that later in the chapter.

Entity Purchase - In this type of Buy-Sell plan, the business is the 'entity' that everything pivots around. It simply states that if a partner dies, becomes incapacitated or retires, the company will buy out their share with the funds being paid to the departing owner or their estate. The remaining partners will see their share in the company increase accordingly. If there are more than two owners, companies often prefer to use this method because if insurance is being used for funding purposes, Entity Purchase cuts down on the number of policies needed. In the Cross Purchase, three partners would have a total of six insurance policies, two each. In the Entity Purchase method, the company would have one policy on each partner or a total of three. So for that very critical area of funding, there is a good reason to lean toward Entity Purchase with three or more partners.

One-Way - Just as the name suggests, this method is used when there is just one owner. I have found that many individual business owners don't think that a Buy-Sell can help them because they do not have a partner to be concerned about taking over the business if something unexpected happens to them. Where a One-Way comes into play is when a business owner has one or more employees, or perhaps a family member (children), that may be interested in buying the business and carrying it on when the owner exits due to death, incapacitation or retirement. Or if the business owner has a solid, already identified, outside suitor for the business. By having a One-Way in place, the person(s) who is interested in buying is put at the front of the line and also can make pre-arrangements with the business owner for funding options.

As I mentioned several times in the above descriptions, 'funding' is a key component to making a Buy-Sell arrangement work. You can have the greatest, most iron-clad legal document in place as to what is *supposed* to happen if a partner were to die, get hurt, retire, etc., but if there is no viable source of funding in place for the surviving partner to compensate the departing partner or their heirs, it is useless.

A great example of a One-Way Buy-Sell is a business owner that I worked with recently. He owns a small business that is five years old and is growing and the future looks very bright. He is in his late 40's and has two employees, both of whom have an interest in buying the business should the owner depart. The owner has no spouse or children but he does have two siblings that he'd like to leave the business to. However, the siblings have no interest in running the business and since it is a specialized product, they are not qualified to handle it anyway. So, how would this owner secure the value of his business to his estate, while making it possible for the employees to buy the company?

Solution: A One-Way Buy-Sell funded with life & disability insurance. The insurance can be set up in a number of ways so that the financial burden does not fall on the employees and that it allows for some business deduction tax advantages as well. If something happens to the owner, the beneficiaries are the employees but due to the Buy-Sell agreement, they must use those funds to buy the business from the siblings to whom it has been left. It would also be spelled out in the Buy-Sell that the siblings are required to sell to the employees. This owner also needs to do proper Succession Planning to prepare the two employees for the added responsibilities they will eventually take on. For this part, it is never too early to start that training because you never know what life has planned around the next corner. It also provides 'buy-in' which is good for morale & company culture.

Here are the primary funding types and what they would cost comparatively. For this example, we are making the assumption that we would need $1,000,000 to buy out our partner and are evaluating the cost over 15 years.

<u>Cash</u> - Cash is cash. Aside from inflationary effects, which I am not going to factor in, if the surviving partner has $1,000,000 in cash then it will cost him $1,000,000 for the buyout.

<u>Borrow</u> - $1,186,982 would be the cost for the buyout. This is based on five equal payments of $200,000 plus interest at 6%.

<u>Sinking Fund</u> - The cost of this method would be $928,379 assuming you stashed away what you would pay for life insurance and it makes 8% along the way. But it would still require a balance of $853,379 in cash.

<u>Life Insurance</u> - $75,000 based on estimated premiums of $5,000 annually for a 45 year-old male, preferred, non-smoker. This would be a Universal Life policy that would accrue cash value making it flexible based on the reason the partner leaves the business.

<u>Disability Buyout Insurance</u> - $76,395 based on estimated premiums of $5,093 for a 45-year old male, Executive Occupation class. Most people don't know this but we are 2 1/2 to 3 times more likely to become incapacitated than we are to die prematurely so this is a very valuable tool in the Buy-Sell agreement process.

Buy-Sell agreements are a critical part of planning in the event that something unexpected happens to a key person(s) in your business. We all hope that nothing happens to us or any of our colleagues but 'hope' is not a solid business strategy. 'Planning' is the single biggest reason that businesses fail, and one component of that planning is succession planning, and a cornerstone of succession planning is a Buy-Sell Agreement.

8. GOT A KEY PERSON?

Vince owns what is now a very large commercial construction company. Back in 2008, Vince hired Mark, a highly regarded, top notch, Civil Engineer and General Sales Manager to take the business to the next level. Over the next eight years, Mark doubled the company's revenue and then doubled it again. With this growth came the need for many more employees, equipment, infrastructure, a full-time Human Resources department and much more. The payroll and benefits the company was now paying out were many times what it had been back in 2008. Mark had done a truly remarkable job to grow the business almost single handily, and there was no doubt in anyone's mind that if anything ever happened to him, there would be a high price to pay. Well, very unfortunately, one night on the way home from a job site his car was struck by another vehicle and he was killed.

Solution: Thankfully, Vince had taken the steps to

protect the business financially from the loss or incapacitation of several key employees, including Mark. Vince had adequate insurance funding on Mark to cover replacing the lost revenue that would occur with him gone, paying the cost of searching for and training Mark's successor and maintaining business continuity for Vince's clients, creditors, and employees.

Just about every business has at least one key person, and usually more, within their company. I'm speaking about employees as well as partners here. We have already addressed protecting ownership of the business in the previous chapter, but now we need to look at what is referred to as 'key people'. These are people whose roles are critical to the success and smooth running of a business. And they can be found in all departments of a company from Sales to Marketing to Finance to Human Resources to Production to Operations, etc..

Many times the importance of certain key people is overlooked in businesses. They are often leaders and establish a standard of proficiency and effort that eventually is taken for granted. The thought of what would happen if they were all of a sudden not around does not occur to people until it is too late.

Key people that contribute to the success and growth of a business have very far reaching effects. Take, for example, Mark, from our story that opened this chapter. Vince hired many more employees to handle the larger work load. That means that many more lives, the employees, AND their families, were now reliant on that paycheck and benefits (healthcare, 401K, dental, IRA, etc.). Consider the fact that with growth, companies also tend to invest more in things like equipment, vehicles, technology and more. So there may be additional business loans that still have to be paid - the banks are not going to interrupt payments because you lost a key person. Likewise, losing a key person may make it more difficult to obtain financing because your revenues are now down, and the prospects for growth are less certain. And last but not least, you as the business owner, and your family are apt to take a big financial hit with a key person loss.

Losing a key person in other areas of the company, like IT, can be equally devastating. If your business is heavily reliant on technology, like perhaps a web based business, and you lose the person that built your platform and knows the system inside and out, it may be almost impossible to recover. That IT person is to your business what Mark was to Vince's construction business. Indispensable.

The point is, you as the business owner should take strong steps to assure the survival of the business in the event that a key person(s) unexpectedly exits. Likely?......maybe not so much statistically. Catastrophic if it happens?.......definitely. It is just prudent to be prepared because there is too much at stake.

The backside of losing a key person is the company recovery. Who replaces the lost person, however they were separated from the company? This is no easy task and is not cheap either. The estimated cost of finding, hiring and training a new employee is roughly 6-9 months salary. So a person making $60,000 might cost his company as much as $45,000 to replace. The cost is less for hourly workers, but much more for executive level employees.

Sometimes it is a matter of a key person deciding they want to jump to another company. Because of this, business owners have also become quite interested in offering customized compensation plans that offer an incentive for key employees to stick around. The longer they stay, the greater the lump payout. And along with these 'deferred compensation' plans, there is also often an added benefit like life insurance and/or disability coverage. So there is an incentive for them to stay as well as protection if something happens to them. The plans and funding have gotten very creative to the point where the net expense to the business, in the long run, is almost nothing. But the savings can be immense.

Key people are in many organizations that most of us probably never think about. Not too long ago I was at an after hours gathering for the Chamber of Commerce I belong to and I got into a conversation about this with our chamber president. He has been there 15 years and does a phenomenal job. He shared with me that the Chamber has both a Key Man insurance policy on him in case something unexpected happens, and they have a deferred compensation plan set up that will offer him a nice lump sum payout after his years of service hit a certain point. That's great planning and it provides for stability in the chamber which ultimately leads to more growth and revenue, and avoids the high expense of searching for, and hiring executive level talent. WIN-WIN.

Other occupations that could justifiably be called 'key people' might include church pastor, association president, private school or college president or other administrative staff, certain members of a Board of Directors, and much, much more.

Taking steps to absorb the loss of key people, as well as putting plans in place to keep the key people in your company for as long as possible, are often overlooked parts of Succession Planning. It all boils down to the 'continuation' of the business if and when something unforeseen arises.

9. Scenarios

Now that we've covered a significant portion of what Succession Planning is, and how it works, I'd like to have you look at several scenarios. There's no need to do anything if you don't want to - I'd just like you to think in your head, based on what you've learned, how these situations could have been addressed with proper planning. Think about a few scenarios that could happen and what the result might be without a Succession Plan and accurate Valuation:

A. The last time you did a valuation on your business was many years ago and the figure was put at $2,000,000. At that time you and your partner had a Cross Purchase Buy-Sell agreement and funded it with two Term Life insurance policies for $1,000,000 each. Tragically, your partner passes away. When the dust settles and your partner's widow's estate attorney steps in, there is a new valuation done on the business whereby they come up with a value figure of $3,000,000. You collect $1,000,000 as the beneficiary of your late partner's life insurance policy, but you still owe his widow $500,000 more. Where does that come from?

B. You and your partner are doing very well with your auto repair business. You have seen similar businesses in your area sell for upwards of $1,000,000 so you are feeling pretty confident that yours is worth a similar amount. Then one day your partner walks in and says that he is getting a divorce from his wife. Now you have two partners. Their divorce is not an amicable one and the wife is demanding her half (1/4) of the business value in cash and your partner just doesn't have $250,000 to hand over to her. Eventually, he tells you that he has no choice but to request you buy him out of his share so he can pay his ex-wife. You don't have $500,000 to give him for his(their) share so the decision is made that the business must be sold. And because of the circumstances and demand for quick cash, a less than fair market price gets accepted.

C. You've grown from just one small seafood restaurant to what is now five locations and all of them are really doing well. Your long range plan of building the restaurant into a great retirement account is working out perfectly. It's working so well, in fact, that at age 65 you think you are ready to exit the business. You have two children and you decide to pass it on to them because they have both been working there for several years, waiting tables and doing various tasks. You wanted them to learn from the school of hard knocks. The two of them are very excited about taking over the business and all of the paperwork is drawn up. You get a valuation done and then establish a payment plan and time line for them to compensate you. Initially, the kids seem to be doing fine but gradually they start to run into problems. The food ordering is a lot more challenging than they thought and they are running out of some of the restaurant favorites. The financial books are a little foreign to them too and they miss some scheduled payments to the bank and to suppliers. Pretty soon the word starts spreading that the restaurant is under new management and things have gone downhill. Sales suffer and before you know it, those payments you are due are getting harder and harder for your kids to make. Eventually, the decision has to be made to sell the restaurant so that there won't be any more losses.

These scenarios are hypothetical but happen

every day in businesses across the country. Nobody thinks it will happen to them - it's going to happen to the other guy. Remember that? Who's the other guy? Do you think the owners and partners in these three hypothetical cases would have felt that spending a modest amount on a solid Succession Plan would have been worth it after they went through their situations? As I said, 'pain points' in succession scenarios don't reveal themselves until it's <u>too late.</u>

Succession Planning Checklist:

Here is a potential check list of items to consider when initiating or updating your succession plans. This list could go on for pages but I have tried to keep it simple and manageable.

_____ Have you identified what your ultimate exit goal for the business is? (page 23)

    _____ Have you established a time frame?

    _____ Do you have partner(s) that needs to be in agreement on this goal?

    _____ Are you taking the proper personal financial planning steps?

_____ Is the goal is to pass the business on to family members? (page 23)

    _____ Are those family members currently working in the business?

    _____ Have you discussed passing on the business with them?

    _____ Is there a plan in place to train the family members on all aspects of the business?

    _____ Is there a contingency plan if the family member(s) change their mind?

_____ Is the goal to sell the business to an employee(s)? (page 23)

    _____ Does the employee want to buy the business? Has it been discussed?

    _____ Does the employee have the financial means or plan to be able to buy?

    _____ Is the employee being trained in all aspects of the business?

    _____ Will the other employees be receptive to this new owner?

    _____ Is there a contingency plan if the employee changes his/her mind?

_____ Is the goal to sell the business to an outside buyer? (page 23)

    _____ Are the necessary steps being taken to establish a great company legacy?

        _____ Company Culture?

        _____ Financial books in order?

        _____ Clean, orderly work environment?

        _____ Latest technology in use?

        _____ State of the art products and production?

_____ Are there KEY employees that are critical to the success of the company? (page 49)

    _____ Is protection in place for the company in the case of physical loss?

_____ Have steps been taken to entice key employee(s) to stay?

_____ Have replacements of key employees been identified?

_____ Have discussions with key employee successors taken place?

_____ Do you know what the accurate value of the company is? (page 34)

_____ Have you had a valuation done in the last two years?

_____ If not, do you have a valuation formula in place? Is it written?

_____ Does it take into account any changes that have taken place in the business?

_____ Is there a Buy-Sell Agreement in place? (page 41)

_____ Is it up to date?

_____ Does it reflect the current valuation of the business?

_____ Does it address the current personal situation of all partners?

_____ Does is reflect any company changes that have taken place?

10. 'Someday' Never Comes

I was contemplating what I wanted to call the last chapter of this short book when it finally came to me. I was working around my yard one day and listening to music from my iPhone which I usually do. One of the great classic Rock & Roll bands, Credence Clearwater Revival, gave me my answer. Credence released a song in 1972 called "Someday Never Comes" and it seemed like an appropriate chapter title to wrap this up.

How many things in our lives have we said that we need to do 'someday'. Someday I need to start exercising more. Someday I will go on a diet. Someday I will give up sugar, or at least cut down on it. That's my big one. Someday we will take a trip out West. Someday I am going to call that old high school friend. We all do it - it is human nature.

They say that people don't make a move, decision

or purchase something unless it addresses a 'pain point' for them. Examples of 'pain points' within a business might be something that is costing you money, something that has a negative effect on productivity, a personnel issue, etc. When it comes to succession planning, the pain points are very different in scope, type, and timing. In business, when you hit a pain point related to succession planning or lack thereof, it is probably too late to do anything about it. It's either going to cost you a lot of time, money, heartache or in many cases, all three! And it could also cost you your business!

Succession planning is something that most business owners acknowledge is something they should do. They've been made aware of it if they have received any business training or legal advice, or read any books on starting their own business. But because it is not part of the day to day activity of growing their company and their bottom line, it is very often overlooked. In fact, documentable figures indicate that over 70% of business owners have not done succession planning. Informal figures, those that I have solicited from professional acquaintances of mine who work in this world (Attorneys, CPA's, Commercial Insurance, etc.) say that the figure is probably closer to 90%.

What are the reasons? There are three that jump

out.

1. "It costs too much" - the two main components that carry a cost when setting up succession planning, aside from funding, are the attorney's fee for a buy-sell or other type of ownership agreement, and the accountant fee to have a valuation done. Typically, these fees would run in the $3-5,000 and $5-10,000 range respectively. However, I can show you a way to get the legal fees down to as little as $1,000 and the valuation cost down to $0! And these services will be provided by top tier professionals in your area, not online templates and software packages.

2. "It takes up too much time" - with all that you have to do as a busy business owner, it is easy to see why you would feel this way. However, when you consider the amount of time, expense & emotional toll that an adverse event can have on your business, you'd have to agree that investing a couple of hours up front makes much more sense. Additionally, for a nominal cost, it is easy to hire a person to handle the majority of the logistics of this type of planning.

3. "It won't happen to me" - hope & luck are not good strategies when it comes to perhaps your most valuable possession outside of your

family. Many business owners count on their company value as their main retirement vehicle. To gamble that on a 'hope & luck' strategy is not a wise idea.

When I decided to write this book, I had the 70%, or 90%, of business owners in mind. As you read, my family and I have been through a crushing event and I don't wish it on anyone. There were certain steps that could have been taken to prevent or significantly ease the financial burden that fell upon me and my family, but I had not taken them, and I greatly regret that. It is my hope that by putting this book in the hands of as many business owners as possible, at least some of them will see the value and importance of protecting what they have built and will feel that a comprehensive succession plan is needed and justified. I have no illusions that everyone that reads this book will immediately decide to initiate succession planning. I'd be thrilled, but I'd be far more shocked. Rather, I hope that by reading this book business owners have been given something to think about and if not now, at least not too far down the road, they will put some serious thought into succession planning. After all, SOMEDAY NEVER COMES!

I hope this book has been:

1. Easy to read & understand.

2. Educational & informative.

3. Thought provoking.

If you have a business, you need a Valuation, Buy-Sell Agreement & Succession Plan.

Good luck and May The Wind Always Be At Your Back!!

ABOUT THE AUTHOR

Ken Parson lives in Chapel Hill, NC with his wife Lydia. After spending twenty years in sales and management for three Fortune 200 companies, Ken started his own insurance business which is going on 16 years and counting. After seeing what a major health event can do to a business and family personally, Ken set out to help business owners avoid going through what he and his family went through. He has assembled a team of strategic partners that specialize in assisting businesses in Succession Planning, Funding and all of the details associated with this process. His focus is on providing business owners access to the highest quality professionals at a cost that wont hurt their bottom line. Outside of work, Ken likes to play golf, work out and follow sports. He was a high school football coach for 16 years and a high school softball coach for ten years. Ken and his wife have three children and six grandchildren